# WITHDRAWN

| | DATE DUE | | |
|---|---|---|---|
| ne | | | |
| | | | |
| | | | |
| | | | |
| | | | |
| | | | |
| | | | |
| | | | |
| | | | |

# AMYCUS

# MONSTERS OF MYTHOLOGY

## 25 VOLUMES

MONSTERS OF MYTHOLOGY

# AMYCUS

*Bernard Evslin*

**CHELSEA HOUSE PUBLISHERS**

New York    Philadelphia

1989

**EDITOR**
Remmel Nunn

**ART DIRECTOR**
Maria Epes

**PICTURE RESEARCHER**
Susan Quist

**SENIOR DESIGNER**
Marjorie Zaum

**EDITORIAL ASSISTANTS**
Heather Lewis, Mark Rifkin

First Printing

1   3   5   7   9   8   6   4   2


Library of Congress Cataloging-in-Publication Data

Evslin, Bernard.
Amycus.

(Monsters of mythology)
Summary: Recounts the myth of the Amycus, the brass-headed
giant who was summoned by Athena to destroy all who
challenged her authority.
1. Amycus (Greek mythology)—Juvenile literature.
[1. Amycus (Greek mythology)   2. Mythology, Greek]
I. Title. II. Series: Evslin, Bernard. Monsters of
mythology.
BL820.A63E97      1989      398.2'1      88-29928

ISBN 1-55546-240-5

Printed in Singapore

This tale of the brass-headed giant
is dedicated to my son TOM,
whose head is of purest gold

# Characters

## Monsters

| | |
|---|---|
| **Amycus**<br>(AHM ih kuhs) | Giant brass-headed maniac |
| **The Cyclopes**<br>(SY klahps) *sing.*<br>(SY kloh peez) *plur.* | Huge one-eyed smiths, powerful servants of the gods |
| **Brontes**<br>(BRAHN teez) | Amycus's father, the cleverest of the Cyclopes |
| **Ludo**<br>(LOO doh) | Another Cyclops |
| **Wingless Dragons** | Giant flame-spitting lizards |

## Gods

| | |
|---|---|
| **Zeus**<br>(ZOOS) | King of the Gods |
| **Athena**<br>(uh THEE nuh) | Goddess of Wisdom |

| | |
|---|---|
| **Poseidon**<br>(poh SY duhn) | God of the Sea |
| **Hades**<br>(HAY deez) | Ruler of the Dead |
| **Hermes**<br>(HUR meez) | The messenger god |

# Mortals

| | |
|---|---|
| **Castor**<br>(KASS tuhr) | Prince of Sparta, a champion wrestler |
| **Pollux**<br>(POL uhks) | Castor's twin brother, a master boxer |
| **Jason**<br>(JAY suhn) | Exiled young king of Iolcus |
| **Peleus**<br>(PEE lee uhs) | Wicked usurper of Jason's throne |
| **Deucalion**<br>(doo KAY lee on) | A worthy man, survivor of the Great Flood |
| **Pyrrha**<br>(PIHR ah) | Deucalion's wife |
| **Girl on Bebrycos** | |

# Animals

| | |
|---|---|
| **Owl** | Athena's spying bird |

| | |
|---|---|
| **Swordfish** | Agent of the owl |
| **White goat, blue fox black bear, brown bear** | |

# Others

| | |
|---|---|
| **Proteus**<br>(PRO tee uhs) | Poseidon's aide, a minor sea deity who changes shape at will |
| **Liana**<br>(LEE ah nuh) | Amycus's mother, Brontes' wife, a sea nymph |

# Contents

# 1

# The Feud

he brass-headed monster, Amycus, who enslaved so many women and battered so many men to death, was born out of a quarrel between Athena, Goddess of Wisdom, and Poseidon, God of the Sea.

They both wielded tremendous power. *Poseidon* means "earth shaker," and he deserved the name; his wrath was catastrophe. And the tall, free-striding Athena who bore spear and shield and whose gray eyes could freeze the marrow of any human and many Olympians was the most feared of all the goddesses.

Their feud had simmered for centuries. It began when Athena, trying to read the future, guessed that a certain small fishing village would grow into a great and brilliant city whose name would be as a song amid the horrid shrieks of history. And she decided that this village of high destiny must call itself after her so that the sound of her name would fall sweetly upon the ear after the other gods were forgotten.

But Poseidon believed that he alone ruled the destinies of all who dwelt along his shores and drew their bounty from his seas. All coastal cities were his, all fishing villages. When pleased,

*The tall, free-striding Athena . . was the most feared of all the goddesses.*

he would send rich harvests of fish; when angered he would crush ships like walnuts, or send storms that swept all who displeased him into the sea. When he discovered that Athena was paying unusual attention to one fishing village he became very angry.

Green robed, green bearded, he loomed over the little huts like a tidal wave about to break. The people gaped in horror. His voice, pounding like the surf, forced them to their knees. He demanded that the village be given his name. Otherwise, he declared, he would starve them by withdrawing fish from their waters, send storms to wreck their ships, sea serpents to devour whoever jumped overboard, and pirates to slaughter anyone left on shore.

Before he departed, the terrified villagers vowed to do whatever he asked.

The clouds split. An arch of sunlight bridged sky and earth, and something strode down the span of light: a maiden goddess, bearing spear and shield. She towered above the village, but her voice was a mighty music and uttered no threats.

"Villagers," she said. "This is the first day of your glorious destiny. I am Athena, daughter of Zeus. I come to offer you my favor forever and to honor you with the gift of my name. Under my blessing shall this cluster of huts grow into a marble city, famed for wit, wisdom, and skill in warfare—which of course brings wealth. So arise, lucky ones, get up off your knees. Stand proud. Under my protection shall you survive and prosper despite all the threats of blowhard Poseidon."

Hearing the musical voice utter these words, gazing upon the stern, radiant goddess, the villagers felt their spirits soar, and decided to ignore the threats of Poseidon.

"Yes!" they cried. "All honor, Great Goddess, all worship! We shall call our village by your name."

And from that time on, both gods sought to fulfill threat and promise. Poseidon never stopped tormenting the Athenians, and Athena sought always to protect them. And the feud between powerful niece and stormy uncle grew more and more vicious, and was to entangle many lives, to cause a horde of deaths, and to spawn a multitude of monsters—the worst of whom, perhaps, was the Horrible Head, also known as Amycus.

# 2

## The Crater

ow, everything about Poseidon irritated Athena, but she was particularly annoyed by his arrogance. All the gods had tremendous opinions of themselves. They all strode proudly and seemed to glow with a sense of being exactly who they were and no one else. But to the eye of his brooding niece, Poseidon seemed to swagger more and be puffed up with the idea of his own importance more than any other god. Worst of all though, Athena thought bitterly, her obnoxious uncle had cause to exult.

For of all the prayers that thronged the air and mounted to heaven, the most frequent and most passionate were those addressed to Poseidon. There was good reason for this. Those who worshiped the Olympians were largely seagoing people—sailors, fisherfolk, pirates. Before every voyage they visited Poseidon's driftwood altars and sacrificed to him, and prayed for fair weather and following winds and safe landfalls. And when, very frequently, the god turned contrary and sent storms and killer tides and savage sea raiders, then, instead of losing faith, the voyagers were terrified into deeper belief, and their prayers grew more fervent than ever.

Athena, studying this, felt her hatred growing so fast she thought she must burst. But she was intelligent enough to learn from what displeased her, and she told herself that the way to injure Poseidon was to make his worshipers lose faith in his powers. And the way to do this was to intensify the peril, to plant special monstrous dangers upon the sea—creatures and events that would destroy ships and crews, and finally teach humankind that the richest sacrifices and most heartfelt prayers to the sea god would not keep them from harm.

This would not be an easy process, she knew; it would take a long time and much skillful plotting . . . flotillas of ships sent to the bottom and hordes of sailors to be drowned, or to meet even worse death. With so much to do then, she set to work immediately.

Athena was known as the wise one not only because she reasoned brilliantly and inspired men like Daedalus to invent the wheel and the plow and the rudder, but because she seemed to know everything about everyone. Indeed, she went to a great deal of trouble to gather this information, training her pet owl to spy upon all the gods and certain humans.

The owl with its silent, gliding wings, its night-piercing eyes, and ears that could pick up the fall of a distant leaf, was perfectly framed for spying—particularly at night, when most secret things are done. And by day a flock of crows, instructed by the owl herself, flew here and there, spying, prying, noticing, and reporting back to the owl, who sifted the information and brought the interesting bits back to Athena. For among its many tricks the clever bird could also speak Greek.

Upon a certain day the owl flew up to Olympus, found Athena, perched on her shoulder and spoke into her ear.

"Oh Goddess, a crow has flown all the way from Sicily to tell me that Mount Aetna is erupting."

"Nonsense," said Athena. "It's forbidden to erupt. Zeus

himself quenched the fires of that raging mountain, hollowed it out and presented it to his son, Hephaestus, to use as a smithy. Therein labor the Cyclopes who forge thunderbolts for Zeus, and weapons and armor and ornaments for the rest of us."

"Nevertheless," said the owl, "the mountain is belching red smoke, and trembling so hard that huge boulders are rolling down its flanks toward the villages below. And all who dwell there are fleeing that part of Sicily."

"It will not erupt, it cannot erupt," said Athena. "What's happening, no doubt, is that the Cyclopes are fighting again. They do that now and then. They're so incredibly strong and their tempers so savage that they sometimes stop working and use their mallets on each other. The fallen ones are flung into the forge fires; therefore does the mountain belch red smoke. And Aetna shakes when the Cyclopes do battle, and rocks roll down its slopes. When Hephaestus arrives and decrees a truce, the Cyclopes will stop fighting and the mountain will stop trembling."

"That may be so, Goddess. But the villagers are still fleeing, and there is great grief and confusion upon the land."

"I shall go there myself and calm them," said Athena.

Whereupon she flew to Sicily and laid a sweet swoon upon the fleeing villagers, and appeared to each of them in the form of a dream, promising them that Aetna would not erupt and that they might return to their homes and dwell in safety.

The villagers awoke, rejoicing. Right there in the field where the strange sleep had overtaken them, they built altars to Athena and Hephaestus and loaded them with fruit and flowers. Singing songs of praise, they returned to their homes.

Athena lingered in Sicily, enjoying the prayers of thanksgiving and the hymns of praise. "Since we're here," she said to her owl, "we'll go and visit that famous smithy. I've never seen the Cyclopes at work and I'm curious about them."

The smoke from the mountain mingled with the morning

mists as Athena approached. Making herself invisible, she flew up to the crater, then floated gently down into it, down through darkening air into the great smithy that was the workshop of Hephaestus.

It was an enormous chamber, taking up the whole inside of the mountain. For Aetna was just a shell. Ages before, when it was an active volcano, earth's primal fire had eaten up through its roots, melting its rocky guts—which had then spewed out as red-hot lava. After Zeus quenched the flames with a sudden torrent of rain that had flooded the entire countryside, he had ordered the Cyclopes to hollow out the rest of the mountain, informing them that this was to be their home and their workplace forevermore.

Athena knew all this, of course; it was family history, but she had never actually visited the smithy before. Now she stared about in amazement. The Cyclopes, male and female, were tall as trees and their half-naked bodies writhed with muscle as they moved about their gigantic labor of forging thunderbolts for Zeus, and weapons and armor for the other gods. The hafts of their sledges were oak trunks, peeled of bark and trimmed of branches. The sledge heads were thousand-pound lumps of fire-tempered iron. And they swung these stupendous mallets like tack hammers.

Not all of them were working at the anvils. Some were making charcoal, tossing whole uprooted trees into the flames. Others were using shovels as big as skiffs, scooping up the charcoal and using it to feed the forge fires, which had to be coal fed to melt metal.

The noise would have shattered the eardrums of anyone who was not a god or goddess. The clanging of sledge against anvil, the crackle of the flames and the wild yelling of the Cyclopes made the loudest clamor Athena had ever heard. But she did not mind it at all. The scene was too fascinating, as interesting as a battle, or an earthquake or tidal wave. For Athena doted on violence, and moved among dire events as easily as a gull riding storm winds.

Unseen by anyone, she slid through the smoke toward one young Cyclops and studied him as he worked. Even his maimed head set upon those magnificent shoulders seemed splendid to her. The single eye embedded in the middle of his forehead was as large as two eyes—big and lustrous, full of innocent savagery like a tiger's eye—but glowing with a kind of proud pain known only to those who feel themselves different from everyone else.

She watched him as he

*The Cyclopes . . . writhed with muscle as they moved about their gigantic labor . . .*

swung his sledge, shaping a red-hot bar of metal. He laid down his sledge, picked up a pair of tongs, nipped the bar, and dipped it into a bucket of water. Steam hissed up, veiling his body. When the steam cleared, he was oiled with sweat and shone like a newly gilded statue. He dropped his tongs and with one hand swung up an enormous keg of water—put it to his lips and drank it all down in one long swallow. He cast the keg aside, picked up a full one and emptied it over his head, drenching himself. Laughing, he wrung out his hair, then picked up his sledge again.

Athena was known for her icy calm in all situations. Now, however, she felt herself being torn by strange feelings. Suddenly, she knew she had to stop breathing this smoky air; it was choking her. With her, as with all gods, wish was action. She wafted herself up, up through sooty shadows, up through the crater and out onto a slope of Aetna.

Athena kept thinking of the Cyclopes after she left the smithy. "They must be the strongest creatures in all the world," she said to herself. "More powerful than the Titans, who are their closest kin. Oh, how I'd like to have an island full of them, right in the middle of Poseidon's sea. I'd be able to do so much with them. I'd inflame their appetites, implant them with so gluttonous a craving for meat that they would devour all the cattle on their island and turn to cannibalism—swimming out to capsize ships, plucking the sailors out of the water and eating them raw. Oh, what a menace to shipping they'd be. More so even than the Sirens perching on jagged rocks, calling sailors to drown. More destructive than my witch, Circe, who lures entire ships' companies into her castle and turns them into swine. . . . Yes, they work well, Circe and the Sirens, and have done me good service. But these Cyclopes, if I can only get them somehow, would destroy more ships and crews than all the rest of my monsters put together . . . But how can I persuade them to leave their smithy? They are creatures of habit and have labored there for thousands of years. I must think very hard about this . . ."

The goddess stood near the top of the mountain, gazing across a sunstruck plain toward a silver glimmer of sea. The sound of mallets striking anvils drifted from the crater; filtered by rock, they chimed like bells. Thinking very hard, she spun one plan after another. One after another, she discarded them. As she pondered, one picture kept flashing in her head: the huge, sweaty young smith hoisting a heavy keg of water and gulping it down, tossing that keg aside, lifting another and pouring it over his head, the grimed one-eyed face grinning under the cascade.

"They work amid flame," she murmured. "They breathe smoke and charcoal dust. Coolness must they crave. Every pore of their parched hides must lust for moisture. Yes-s-s, that giant lad with his buckets gives me a clue."

She knew what she wanted to do now, but she had to wait until nightfall. When the moon had climbed and waned and the

*The Cyclopes felt their salt blood dance in their veins,
pulling them out of the crater toward the shore.*

chiming of hammers had ceased, she knew that the Cyclopes slept. She stretched her arms and turned slowly, weaving a spell. The owl rose from her shoulder and hovered over her head, pivoting in the air as the goddess turned on the grass.

Athena sent the Cyclopes cool dreams. She slid seascape visions through the crater into their sleep: swirling tides, foam-laced waves, and the changing colors of the deep as the sun sifted through water—jade green on top, turning blue, becoming purple, then blue-black, all of it cold, cold, colder. She shuffled dreams all night long, one seascape after another. The older Cyclopes awoke refreshed and went to work immediately. But the younger ones were tangled in their dreams and couldn't cast them off. Nor did they wish to. Overnight their smithy had become loathsome to them. They felt they could not breathe one more breath of the hot smoky air. The blue core of the forge fire became flickers of the blue sea. They felt their salt blood dance in their veins, pulling them out of the crater toward the shore.

# 3

# Owl and Seal

ndeed, twelve young Cyclopes did find themselves entangled in their cool dreams when they awoke the next morning. They looked about the great sooty chamber and couldn't believe that they had consented to spend so much of their life there, and were expected to labor there through eternity. They studied the waiting anvils, the smouldering forge fires, the sullen heaps of charcoal; they gazed upon the other Cyclopes still sunk in slumber. It all made no sense to them; only their sea dream seemed real.

"Let's do it," muttered one named Brontes. He was the giant youth who had doused himself with water as Athena watched. He picked up his mallet and strode out of the smithy and the others followed. They filed through a chain of linked caves; the final one opened out upon a slope of Aetna, near its base.

Athena, still perched near the top of the mountain, heard them shouting as they burst out of the cave. She looked down and saw them running off the slope, into the forest. She watched them as they disappeared into the woods, and listened to their wild yelling as if it were music. For the goddess knew that her magic was working, that she had cast her dream as skillfully as a fisherman casting his net—that she had caught the Cyclopes in her vision, and that they were being pulled toward the sea.

In that part of Sicily, then, the woods ran right down to a strip of beach. Brontes stopped at the fringe of the forest, laid down his mallet, wrapped his arms about the trunk of a tree and began to pull. Straining every muscle, he tried to wrench it out of the ground. This tree was well grown and had a deep root system. But Brontes, in the early prime of his enormous strength made even stronger by joy, pulled the roots right out of the

*In that part of Sicily, then, the woods ran*
*right down to a strip of beach.*

clinging earth, and cast the tree on the beach. Each of his comrades was also uprooting a tree. When twelve trees lay on the beach, Cyclopes lashed them together with vines and made a huge, heavy raft.

They lifted the raft, ran into the surf, and jumped aboard, rowing with their mallets. Now, a raft is the clumsiest of all vessels and extremely hard to move the way you want it to go. And this raft was probably the largest ever made. But with six Cyclopes rowing on each side, the ponderous wooden platform skimmed across the chop like a canoe.

Athena, who had followed them through the forest and watched them launch the raft, now set off for Olympus, chuckling. She knew that they would find an island and drive out whoever dwelt there. "Once they devour all the game on the island," she said to her owl, "I'll send them cannibal dreams and implant in them a ravening appetite for human flesh. I'll slide scenes of shipwreck into their slumber and show them pictures of themselves fishing sailors out and barbecuing them over a driftwood fire. Once they get the yen, they'll not wait for storms, but swim out and capsize their own ships, and swim home with pockets full of sailors . . . Fly after them," she said to the owl, "and see where they land, so that I'll know what island to visit when the time comes. I'd like to follow them myself, but I have to go to Athens now and inspire young Daedalus with the idea for a hinged steering board to be called a rudder and which will take the place of the awkward sweep oars used now. This device will allow ships to be managed more easily and give seamen more confidence in themselves so that they will depend less on the favor of that puffed-up windbag, Poseidon. So off with you, Owl, and follow my Cyclopes until they make landfall."

As it happened, though, Athena would have done better not sending the owl. For the Cyclopes' raft had been sighted by a creature called Proteus, who served Poseidon, and served him well. He made an admirable spy because he could change shape

*The Cyclopes' raft had been sighted by a creature called Proteus, who served Poseidon and served him well.*

at will and was very sharp-witted and observant in whatever body he chose to use. Now, in his favorite form of white seal, he was circling the raft, studying the Cyclopes, and wondering what had brought them out of the crater and into the sea. Then he spotted the owl hovering over the raft.

"Athena's bird!" he exclaimed to himself. "Which means that her spiteful mistress is mixed up somehow with this mysterious raft. Which, in turn, means that it's part of some plot against my master. For the owl goddess loathes Poseidon, and seeks every opportunity to damage his reputation and rob him of worshipers . . . I'll tell him immediately."

But seals can swim only a certain distance underwater. So Proteus changed himself into a barracuda, and streaked into the ocean depths. Through darkening fathoms he flashed, to the deepest part of the Middle Sea where Poseidon had built his castle. It was a magnificent pile of coral and pearl.

He found Poseidon sitting on his walrus-ivory throne and clove the water toward him, scattering Nereids as he swam. For sea nymphs swarmed about their green-bearded king like minnows about a crust of bread.

"Oh Master," he cried. "I have seen a strangeness afloat! A crew of Cyclopes rowing a great raft somewhere with their mallets—and following them, Athena's own owl."

"Athena!" shouted the sea god, twirling his trident. "Is that armored bitch up to her foul tricks again? Has she sent forth these one-eyed giants to disrupt shipping in some way and strip seamen of faith in their great protector—namely, me? I have no idea how she intends to use them, but whatever she intends, I'll see that she's thwarted. I'll guide their raft into a riptide and drown them all . . . No . . . I've always admired the Cyclopes and the work they do. I've always wished I could have a few of them working for me. I have vaults full of silver and gold, and heaps of jewels from the holds of sunken treasure ships—and I have no one to work this precious stuff. Yes, I'd very much like to have a band of titanic smiths working for me, beating out gorgeous trinkets that I could pass out as favors to these sweet Nereids that cluster about my throne. Yes, and larger and more gorgeous necklaces and rings and brooches and bracelets for my wife, Amphitrite, so that she might overlook my gifts to the sea nymphs. Yes, yes . . . I'll send my riptide, but not to drown them. I'll draw them down here. I'll give them an underwater cave for their smithy. What a splendid idea! How brilliant I am today! And how furious that stupid Goddess of Wisdom will be when she learns that I've turned her plot against her and that the one-eyed giants are working for me. Thank you, Proteus, you have brought me valuable information today, oh Changeable One."

"All my changes," said Proteus, "have but one theme: to serve my master."

He became an eel, a dangerous kind, and touched his electric tail to a few sea nymphs, of whom he was jealous, shocking them, making them quiver and yelp. Then he sped away before they could catch him.

# 4

# The Crystal Smithy

t all happened as Poseidon had decreed. He sent a riptide that spun the huge raft like a twig. The Cyclopes went flying off into the water, were gripped by the riptide and sucked down to the bottom of the sea.

They lost consciousness as they sank, and awoke in a great underwater chamber full of filtered green light. The walls of the chamber were pure crystal. Beyond the walls glided silent fish, big ones and little ones, shark and octopi, balloon fish, rainbow fish, sea turtles as large as the lost raft, and tiny flickering red sparks of fish—and a school of green-haired Nereids. The lovely lithe young sea nymphs shouldered the fish away from the crystal walls and smiled in at the Cyclopes—who were convinced that they were still caught in a dream.

For those who wield strange powers and are familiar with enchantments, there is only a thin membrane between dream and reality, because the most potent dreams are wishes told in code. And for the Cyclopes, for Titans, Olympians, petty gods and demons, and all who are god kin, wish immediately becomes deed—or tries to. So to the Cyclopes, who had been enmeshed in the sea dream sent by Athena and had deserted their crater in Aetna, what happened afterward became part of the same dream. The raft, the riptide, the swooning plunge, and now the crystal chamber with its filtered green light, the wonderful healing coolness, the goggling fishes and the smiling sea nymphs—were all part of a shared dream into which they were sinking deeper and deeper.

It was perfectly natural then for them to see anvils sprouting like mushrooms from the floor of their chamber. An anvil for each . . . and beside each anvil a chest full of gold and silver. And beside each chest a tall coral branch hung with rubies and diamonds and sapphires. No forge fires here in this magic cool smithy. For they were not required to work crude slags of iron here, heating the bars red hot, then hammering them out. No, silver and gold were softer metals, ingots that the Cyclopes could take into their enormously strong hands and twist into any shape they desired. For they understood immediately that they were to make ornaments now, not spears or swords or thunderbolts— that with beautiful work they would pay for coolness and fathoms of space and sea nymph smiles.

Natural . . . it all seemed natural and fitting. Are not sprouting anvils and sudden treasure chests the ordinary furniture of dreams?

Now in the Aetna workshop Brontes had been able to swing his heavy mallet all day while allowing his mind to drift, but here in the crystal smithy he had to concentrate as he twisted gold and silver into delicate ornaments. Upon this certain day he was stringing diamonds and pearls onto a gold wire and didn't see the Nereid until she was standing near his bench.

He gaped at her in wonder. Before this he had only seen the nymphs as they swam or floated beyond the crystal walls— seen them lying in the water, or darting through, bodies tilted. Now here was one standing before him, and she was very close. Nor was she smiling; she was regarding him gravely, and was so beautiful that Brontes found himself unable to breathe. The great bellows of his chest rose and fell, but he felt that he was suffocating. He reached for her; she glided away.

"Are you a monster?" she murmured.

"I am a Cyclops, cousin to the gods."

"You look like a monster, though. Big and strong—which is nice. But monstrously ugly."

"Our great-grandparents were born of Uranus and Gaia, who were grandparents to the Olympians, including your own Poseidon . . . But I'm sorry you think I'm ugly, because I think you're beautiful."

"Well, you have a terrific build. But that huge single eye in the middle of your forehead rather mars your appearance, don't you think?"

"Wait a second," said Brontes.

"What for?"

"I mean to please you more than I do now."

As she watched, he snatched up a gold ingot and squashed it in his mighty hands, pressing it into a sphere, slightly

*"Are you a monster?"*
*she murmured.*

21

*"I am a Cyclops, cousin to the gods."*

larger than his head. He put the shining sphere on his anvil and smashed his fist into it, driving a hole into it, making it bowl shaped.

"Ludo!" he called.

Another Cyclops came to him. "We're the same head size," said Brontes. "Help me out, will you?"

He balanced the bowl on Ludo's head. The opening wasn't large enough; the bowl sat on top of his head. "This may give you a slight headache," said Brontes. "But I'll do the same for you, if need be."

He lifted his mallet and smashed the great sledge down on the bowl, driving it down over Ludo's face. The Cyclops's legs, thick as tree trunks, trembled a bit, but the muscled column of his neck stayed rigid, holding his head still.

"Work it off now," said Brontes. "Gently . . . gently; it's tight, you'll scratch yourself."

Ludo tried to say something, but his voice was muffled

inside the bowl. He worked it up past his mouth and said, "It's coming off easily; it's slippery with blood."

The sea nymph gasped as he pulled the bowl off. Blood gushed from his nose; his lips were cut.

"Thank you," said Brontes.

Ludo nodded and walked away. Brontes dipped the bowl into a bucket of water, washing out the blood. Then he took an awl and punched out two eyeholes. With his powerful fingers he pinched a nose shape under the eyes, and poked two nostril holes. With his thumbnail, stronger and sharper than any knife blade, he cut out a mouth. He studied a large sapphire, and sliced it into a pair of lenses, which he stuck into the eyeholes.

Now a golden head stood on the anvil. He picked it up and pulled it over his own head. It fit exactly. And the nymph gazed in admiration at the giant upon whose shoulders sat a magnificent golden head. Brontes laughed with pleasure as he saw her expression. He took her by the waist and lifted her until her eyes were level with his glittering sapphire ones.

"Be careful how you kiss me," she whispered. "I bruise easily."

# 5

# A Monster Is Born

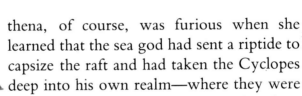thena, of course, was furious when she learned that the sea god had sent a riptide to capsize the raft and had taken the Cyclopes deep into his own realm—where they were now doing his work. She couldn't endure the thought that these one-eyed giants, whom she had tempted out of Aetna to disrupt shipping and damage Poseidon's reputation, were now actually serving her enemy. For all her hot temper, though, Athena never allowed anger to scatter her wits, and she immediately began to plan some kind of counterattack.

But she didn't quite know what to do because she lacked exact information about what was happening below. Nor could she send her owl. But the canny bird was very good at reading Athena's wishes.

"Oh Mistress," she said. "Forgive me, but I have acted without orders."

"What do you mean?" asked Athena.

"Well, I knew that you would want to know just what was happening down there in that crystal smithy where the Cyclopes now dwell, and I also knew that I was useless to you underwater, for I drown easily. So I made bold to act in your name. I found a spiteful swordfish, a fine, big, sleek fellow but very resentful of things because, in a fury of greed, he had mistaken a mossy rock for a manta ray, had tried to stab it to death and broken his sword. Now he's unable to duel the other fish or do much hunting, and he's mean and hungry. I asked him to do his swimming about the crystal chamber, to observe what was happening, to surface and to report everything to me. In return for his spying, I said you would fit him out with a brand-new sword."

"I am very pleased with you," said Athena. "How often will he report to you?"

"I'll give him a week to learn what he can, then I'll fly out to meet him. After that, it will be every few days."

"Good, good," said Athena. "Let me know immediately if you learn anything."

Some days later, the owl flew back to Olympus, sat on Athena's shoulder and whispered, "Important news, oh Goddess."

"Speak, speak . . . "

"It seems that a Nereid named Liana has caused Brontes to fall violently in love with her."

"Those Cyclopes do everything violently," said Athena. "Does she love him in return?"

"Seems to."

"How is it possible? He's so ugly. They all are."

"He has improved himself," said the owl. "He has made himself a golden head with sapphire eyes. It slips over his own head and makes him look quite splendid."

"Where do they meet? Inside the crystal smithy, among all the forges?"

"That's where they first met," said the owl. "But now, needing privacy, he slips out of the smithy and swims with her. He's a very powerful swimmer, of course, and she has taught him to breathe underwater. This my swordfish has told me. At first I thought he might be making it up just to have something interesting to tell; then I realized that he doesn't have the imagination for so gorgeous a lie, and that it must all be true. By the way, he'd like his new blade as soon as possible. When can he have it?"

"Not quite yet," said Athena. "But tell him he has made a fine start, that I am pleased, and that if he keeps up the good work he should have his sword soon. One that will not break, incidentally, no matter how many rocks he wants to stab."

Every few days, the owl left Olympus and flew over the changing waters until she reached the appointed spot and hovered there until the glittering fish lanced out of the sea. She dropped down to meet him, and he told her all that he had seen. Then she flew back to the sacred mountain. After the third such meeting she came to Athena, bursting with news.

"Oh Goddess," she cried, "they're all doing it now!"

"Who's doing what?"

"The Cyclopes down there. They've all made golden heads for themselves and are courting sea nymphs."

*The glittering fish lanced out of the sea . . . and told her all that he had seen.*

"Indeed? Aren't they shirking their labors? Doesn't Poseidon object?"

"Oh no," said the owl. "Love seems to make them work harder than ever. They're making wonderful jewelry for him, and then they work for themselves making pieces for the sea nymphs. And do you know, to check the fish's tale, I flew over the place on a moonless night and saw faery lights dancing in the dark waters as if the whole sea bottom were ablaze. It must be all those golden heads moving down there and the garlands of jewels being flung to joyous nymphs."

"Ah, they're fiery creatures, those Cyclopes," murmured Athena. "Baked first in the earth's buried flames, now working the sea's sunken treasures. Tell me, do they quarrel among themselves at all? I mean, do two of them ever court the same nymph and fight for her favors?"

"So far, no," said the owl. "Only Brontes seems to have some anger smouldering in him. He was not pleased at all when the others began making their own gold heads. I think he thought they might be wanting to impress Liana, you know. And he would growl if any of them even looked at her. But now that every Cyclops has claimed his own Nereid, I suppose Brontes has cooled off."

"Has he?" said Athena. "Well, perhaps. But this gives me the beginning of an idea. And you shall have a reward. The gardener dug up a litter of field mice today, and I made him save them for you."

Now, the owl did not like tame food. She much preferred to catch her dinner for herself—where the intense listening and the silent dive and the pounce and the devouring of whatever she caught in her claws were all part of the same wild savor. Nevertheless, she thanked Athena and flew off to eat the captured mice. For she was much too wise to refuse any gift of the gods—whose generosity so swiftly became rage when they sensed any lack of gratitude.

Athena thought hard about what the owl had told her, and

finally decided what to do. She visited Brontes' sleep and hung pictures of him and Ludo standing at an anvil with Liana between them. But it was Ludo she was smiling at; it was Ludo who wore the newly made golden head. Brontes raised a hand to seize the nymph, but she drifted away and twined herself about Ludo. Brontes flung himself upon them, ready to kill. Ludo swung his mallet. Brontes heard his skull cracking and felt an awful pain. Darkness swarmed.

He awoke into blackness; he didn't know where he was, whether he was dead or alive, awake or asleep. Liana was kneeling to him, stroking his face, murmuring, "Wake up . . . wake up . . . You're having a terrible dream. . . ." And he had to clench one hand in the other to keep from strangling her. It had all been a nightmare, he realized. She had not smiled at Ludo, and Ludo had not struck him with a mallet. Nevertheless, he couldn't shake off his wrath.

He tried to go back to sleep, hoping to cleanse himself of bewilderment and savage pain. As he slept, however, Athena sent another vision. A technical one, this time. She inspired him with invention. She taught him to read certain secrets of metal. In his vision he was standing over a vat of melting copper. Into it he was casting slags of tin. A bright bubble grew from the vat. It was a head, but not of gold, nor of silver, nor of copper or tin. This was some new metal, very bright; when he tapped it with his hammer, he knew that it was hard, hard as iron, but would not rust.

"I name you *Brass*," he said.

He awoke and swam away from Liana, entered his smithy, took copper and tin, and began to smelt them as his dream had taught. He made himself a brass head, and set it with diamond eyes instead of sapphire, for diamonds are harder. Then he strode forth, looking for trouble.

The vision sent by Athena had warped his senses, and made him see what was not there. He became convinced that not only Ludo but every other Cyclops was planning to steal Liana from

*Brontes became convinced that . . .*
*every other Cyclops was*
*planning to steal*
*Liana from him.*

him, and was trying to mislead him by pretending interest in other Nereids. So he decided to get rid of his rivals once and for all.

He moved in a strangeness. Everything had changed. He didn't fight in his usual way, didn't try to smash the others with his enormous fists, or to break bones with his mallet. His dream had laid a magic mandate upon him; the brass head was to be his weapon.

The water heaved as great bodies writhed below. The swordfish made his rounds and sped toward the surface. The owl dipped to meet him. She heard what he had to say, then flew off to Olympus. She perched on Athena's shoulder and poured out her news.

"He butts them, he butts them!" she cried.

"Who's butting whom? What are you talking about?"

"Brontes I'm talking about. He's become a terror among his fellows. He's butting them to pieces. The Cyclopes fight now as stags do, knocking their heads together. And, oh wise Goddess, what you planned is working beautifully. No gold head can take a knock from the brass one. One blow of Brontes' head crushes a golden helm, and no one dares risk a second blow that would pulp any skull. One butt from Brontes and his enemy flees. This has touched off a great migration. The Cyclopes are quitting the underwater smithy as fast as they can. Only Brontes remains."

"Oh glory!" cried Athena. "Just what I wanted! Now I shall guide them to an island I know, right in the path of busy shipping lanes. Once they reach the island I shall starve them into cannibalism. They'll wreck ships and devour the crews. Yes, just as I originally planned. Won't Poseidon be furious? Oh, I shall gloat, gloat, gloat!"

Things did happen that way for a while, and Athena was very happy. So was the swordfish, for he now had a new sword, longer and sharper than the one he had before. He immediately stabbed some of his enemies, plus a few friends, and set out to hunt manta rays.

And this successful plan of Athena's had another consequence, which she hadn't planned, but which also pleased her mightily. Brontes stayed underwater, working for Poseidon and making ornaments for Liana, whom he had forgiven for what she had done in his dream. He wore his brass head so much that it became a natural part of him, and Liana gave birth to a son who had a brass head.

They named him *Amycus*, which means "bellower," for no sooner had the brass-headed babe entered the world than he began to utter hideous loud braying sounds. He grew with monstrous speed; by the time he was three weeks old he was almost as big as his father, and had learned to use his brass head with deadly effect, pounding sharks into jellyfish. Then, much to his parents' relief, he swam away, declaring that the sea was too salty and much too wet, and that he intended to live on dry land.

Athena was delighted to hear about this. "That gruesome babe has possibilities," she told her owl. "Only three weeks old and already a regular monster. How useful he'll be when he reaches his full growth."

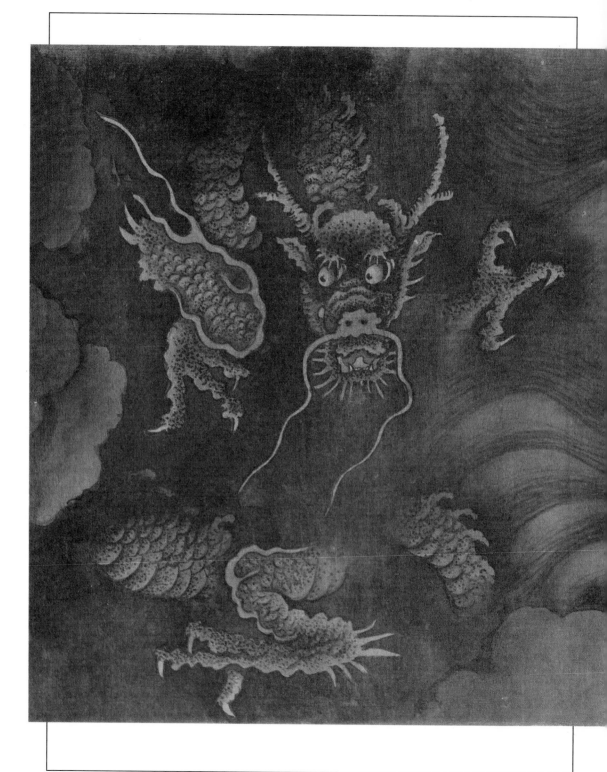

# 6

# Wingless Dragons

uided by Athena, the brass-headed young monster landed on an island called Bebrycos—which had a curious history. Before the Great Flood it had been a mountain standing some twenty miles inland. This was shortly after the human race had been planted on earth, and Zeus was becoming sorry he had done so.

"They're impossible," he declared to the High Council. "They lie as fast as they can talk, help themselves to their neighbors' property, and murder each other wholesale."

"But Sire," said Hermes, who had always been a friend to man, "they only do what we do."

"Perhaps . . ." said Zeus. "But we are gods and know how to forgive ourselves. Our habits, when practiced by mortals, become abominations. I'm going to send a flood of water and wash that foul breed right off the earth."

Whereupon, angry Zeus scooped the oceans out of their beds, and the rivers and the lakes—lifted the mass of water up to heaven and dropped it upon earth in a mighty flood. Cities, towns, and villages were swept away—and farms and sheepfolds, and all the dwellings of man. The Middle Sea doubled its size,

*Angry Zeus . . . lifted the mass of water up to heaven
and dropped it upon earth
in a mighty flood.*

swallowing up great chunks of land whose mountaintops became islands.

Everyone on earth was drowned except a man named Deucalion and his wife, Pyrrha—who were either more virtuous than others, or better swimmers. For the ancient tale tells how the boat built by Deucalion was sucked under, how he and his wife struggled to stay afloat in the raging waters, and were finally deposited, half dead, on the island that had once been the top of Mt. Bebrycos.

The island was lush. The castaways found fruit to eat, springwater to drink. But there were no other people on the island, and, looking out upon the waste of waters, they could see no sail.

"We must build another boat and go to a place where there are other people," said Pyrrha.

"How do you know that there are any people anywhere?"

asked Deucalion. "Perhaps we're the only ones left alive."

"No, it can't be! I can't bear the thought!" cried Pyrrha. "It would be too lonesome that way."

Deucalion could not bear to see his wife suffer. He turned his face to the blank sky and said: "If there be something up there, speak to me, I pray. Tell me if there are any other people on earth. Or are we the last?"

A voice spoke out of the sky. "You are the last. Praise our mercy."

"I thank you for holding our heads above the water," said Deucalion. "Now I ask a further act of mercy. If we are the last people left alive on earth, then take us also. For we cannot bear the loneliness."

There was silence. A great hush filled the world. Even the gulls had stopped calling. Man and wife looked at each other. The voice spoke again.

"Deucalion and Pyrrha, gather the bones of your mother, and as you walk cast them over your shoulders."

"What's that mean?" whispered Pyrrha. "The bones of our mother? We had different mothers. And their bones aren't here anyway."

"The gods speak in riddles sometimes," said Deucalion, "and measure our faith by our ability to unriddle what they say."

"You're speaking in that funny way too," said Pyrrha. "I can't stand it. Tell me plainly—what does he mean by the bones of our mother?"

"Since we do have different mothers, perhaps the voice means a common mother—Mother Earth. But what would be her bones?"

"How about rocks?" said Pyrrha.

"Rocks? . . . Well, we can try."

But rocks were big, and socketed deep in the earth; they couldn't be budged. So they each gathered an armful of stones and walked along the beach casting them over their shoulders.

They heard footsteps behind them, and whirled about. The stones were turning into people. Those Deucalion had cast became men, and women grew from the stones cast by Pyrrha. Twelve men and twelve women, full of wonder and hope and ignorance. And from these twelve men and women were born a new generation.

Bebrycos grew too small for them. The young ones built boats and sailed away, found other islands, and settled there. Found a mainland and settled there.

Generation followed generation, and Zeus sent no more floods. For without people to worship him, he decided, it was hard for him to know that he was a god.

Now, hundreds of years later, as Amycus was plowing the Middle Sea toward Bebrycos, Athena took a journey. She traveled down to Tartarus, to the ebony and fire-ruby castle of her uncle, Hades.

"Welcome, Niece," he said. "It is centuries since you have honored our gloomy precincts with your presence."

"I have come to ask a favor, great Hades."

"Of course," he said. "Why else would anyone come down here who didn't have to? Speak. What is it I can do for you?"

"You will remember, Uncle, that the Great Flood swallowed fifty miles of the Trinacrian coast, including a mountain called Bebrycos, whose highest peaks now form an island. But since it was once a mountain, the roots of this island are still anchored here in Tartarus. And these roots are hollow shafts of rock leading straight up into the caves of the island."

"I hear ancient history and some bits of geology," said Hades. "What do they have to do with the favor you are asking?"

"Patience, my lord. I was describing a natural passageway from your realm to Bebrycos. What I want is to borrow some of your creatures for a hundred years or so. They can climb up through the shafts of rock onto this island, and serve my purpose there. I mean *our* purpose."

"*Our?*" asked Hades. "What possible interest of mine can be served by my creatures above ground?"

"If what you lend me are fearful enough, they will create a horde of fresh corpses, and send new shades thronging down to enlarge your kingdom."

"Interesting . . ." murmured Hades. "Let's see what I can spare. The choices are limited. No Harpies; I need them here. No roasting-pit demons, nor those who wield the fire-flick or the marrow-log; they're all fully employed. I can let you have some general-torment fiends."

"What are they?"

Hades clapped his hands and whistled thrice. Into the throne room shuffled a thing that looked like a wingless dragon. It walked on two legs and stood about eight feet tall. Had green mottled skin as hard as armor, a ridged tail, and crocodile jaws.

"Fire!" barked Hades.

The creature opened its jaws and spat flame.

"Excellent!" cried Athena. "Even better than I imagined. Oh, thank you, Uncle, thank you. How many can I have?"

"Twenty," said Hades. "That's the very best I can do."

"Oh, marvelous!"

"I must warn you," said Hades. "They are witless. They can take no initiative. They must be fully instructed as to whom to kill and how many."

"Suits my purpose exactly," said Athena. "I mean to supply them with a leader, even more murderous, and very intelligent."

*"Fire!" barked Hades.*

"Very well," said Hades. "And when can I be expecting a batch of corpses from Bebrycos?"

"Soon . . . soon . . . " said Athena, and departed, very pleased.

Thus it was that when Amycus swam to shore, he found twenty wingless dragons waiting on the beach. He lowered his head, preparing to fight, but a huge owl dived out of the sky, crying, "No, Amycus, do not attack! These creatures are as useful as they are ugly. They are sent here to serve you and help you to become king of this island."

"Who are you?"

"I serve Athena, the goddess who guides your destiny."

"And I am to be king of this place?"

"And much more. A terror to visitors and castaways, of whom you will be sent multitudes. And a superb menace to shipping. Your name will be spoken with fear as long as tales are told."

"Are these things as fearsome as they look?"

"Even more so. Their claws can rip out an elephant's entrails; their jaws crush the largest bone; their tails can scythe down a thick tree. And . . . they spit fire."

"They do seem well qualified for any fiendish task," said Amycus. "Convey my thanks to the goddess, and tell her that when I am king I shall raise her an altar larger and more splendid than any in the world."

Now, those who dwelt on the island were brave, heavily armed, and skillful fighters. Throughout their history they had fought off vicious pirate raids and resisted invaders from Crete, Carthage, and Mycenae. But their enemies had always been human, and when a band of walking crocodiles led by a brass-headed giant suddenly appeared on their shore, they were confused and frightened. They mastered their fear, however, and marched against the weird invaders.

But when the troops reached the beach and actually saw

what they were supposed to fight, they halted abruptly and tried not to believe what they were seeing—an array of enormous lizards dwarfed by a giant whose head was a ball of blinding light in the noonday sun.

"Listen to me, good folk," roared Amycus. He was trying to speak gently, which meant that he was bellowing a bit more softly than usual. "Before you attack, let me show you what you'll be facing."

He motioned to the dragons, who wheeled and spat flame at a nearby grove of trees. They spat simultaneously. Twenty jets of fire hit the trees, which immediately began to burn. Like tall torches they burned. A flock of birds rose out of the branches, feathers on fire. As the island troops watched, the trees burned to the ground.

"You see?" said Amycus. "If I had turned them the other way, it is you who would be burning. So why don't you just lay down your arms like good little people, and surrender. We'll work you hard, but it's better than burning."

"Never!" cried the battle chief. "Death before slavery!"

"It's all right for you to choose death for yourself," said

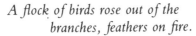

*A flock of birds rose out of the
branches, feathers on fire.*

Amycus, "but why take so many men with you? I'll tell you what I'll do. Search the island through and bring out your best fighters—ten of them, twenty, however many you wish. I'll fight them all at once. If I do not finish them off in an hour, then we'll withdraw peacefully. But if I vanquish your champions, then you'll all surrender, and your lives will be spared."

"Agreed!" cried the battle chief. "The best fighters on the island are those facing you now. I'll choose twenty of them and we can set to work immediately."

"How many in your entire troop?" asked Amycus.

"Fifty-six."

"Make it fifty-six, then," said Amycus. "I'll fight your entire company—and without weapons. Nor shall my greenish friends here do any flamethrowing. But you need not disarm."

*"Charge!" yelled the chief.*

He motioned to the dragons, who slithered away until they were almost out of sight.

"Charge!" yelled the chief.

The islanders attacked. They swarmed over Amycus, striking with sword and battle-ax. He gathered up an armful of the troops, lifted the struggling mass to chin level, and then systematically began to butt. Shield and helmet were like tissue paper before that flailing brass head. Skulls split like eggs, spilling a yolk of brains. When Amycus opened his arms ten corpses fell. The sand soaked up their blood.

But the others did not flee. They were gripped in a battle rage. They kept hacking at him. He pretended to retreat, not fast, for he wished them to follow close. He reached a tree, sprang up and hooked his legs over a massive bough. Hanging upside down, he began to swing. Faster and faster he swung. Now his head was like a wrecking ball, crushing helmets, breastplates, skulls, ribs.

By the time he stopped swinging, half the original troop lay dead, and the other realized how futile it was to contend against this giant. They let their weapons fall, and knelt on the beach.

"You are brave men," bellowed Amycus. "And I spare your lives. Go now and inform the people of the island that they have a new master. And bid them report to me so that I may assign them their tasks."

The men dragged themselves to their feet and shuffled away, knowing that nothing would ever be the same again, and almost envying their comrades who had died too swiftly to feel the bitterness of defeat.

# 7

# The Spartan Twins

ome time before this story begins, Peleus the Proud had seized power in Iolcus by murdering the king. He would have killed the king's three-year-old son also, but the child had vanished on that night of blood and was not found despite a frantic search.

Now Peleus proved to be a very successful battle chief. He sent his troops against his neighbors, scattering their armies, looting their treasuries, and enslaving them. But his paunch grew with his power. He fed gluttonously, insisting on sixteen meals a day without counting snacks, and had grown grossly fat. Seven chins he had, all of them greasy, and his cheeks ballooned so that you could hardly see his tiny pig eyes.

These eyes now were fastened on a pair of twins who stood before the throne. And the king was scowling because he didn't like what he saw. Having grown so gross and ugly himself, he hated the sight of handsome men, and these twins were the most beautiful youths he had ever seen. Very young they looked, scarcely nineteen, but the tallest of the Royal Guard barely reached their shoulders, and these guards had been picked for size—and ugliness. The twins were yellow haired; they blazed with health and strength, and stood easily, not at all troubled by the king's scowls.

Studying them, Peleus saw that they were not quite identical. One was blue eyed; the other had icy gray eyes.

"Who are you?" rasped Peleus. "And what do you want?"

"I'm Castor," said the blue-eyed one. "He's Pollux. We are princes of Sparta."

"And what we want is employment," said the gray-eyed one. "Heralds have been scuttling about, proclaiming that you wish to hire the best fighting men in the lands of the Middle Sea."

"*Men,*" snarled Peleus. "Not pretty puppets who look more like dancing girls than warriors."

The twins smiled an identical smile. "These heavily armed men who patrol this throne room—they are the Royal Guard, are they not?" asked Castor softly.

"They are," said the king.

"Picked for their fighting abilities, no doubt?"

"No doubt."

"Observe," said Castor.

He whirled, seized two guards, one in each hand, and lifted them by the nape of their neck. They struggled, struck at him, tried to kick themselves free, but were helpless as kittens in his hands. Smiling at the king, he knocked their helmeted heads together and flung them, clattering, on the marble floor, where they lay motionless.

"They're not dead," said Castor. "Just out of it for a bit. I was quite gentle. My specialty is wrestling, by the way; my brother's the boxer."

Moving so fast that he was a blur, Pollux wrenched a shield from the hands of another guard, held it in his left hand, drew back his right fist, and punched a hole clean through the heavy bronze buckler. He cast the shield aside and licked his knuckles, which were bleeding slightly. And the twins stood again impassively before the throne, as if nothing had happened.

But the king, for all his girth, had no softness about him. He was not easily flustered.

"Yes, you seem to be able to handle yourselves," he drawled. "Of course, if I employ you, you'll be going against more fearsome foes than these. What's your fee?"

"Depends on what you want us to do," said Castor.

Peleus had been thinking very swiftly all this while. "These baby-faced thugs can prove dangerous as well as useful," he said to himself. "They're just too good at what they do. And much too independent. If they stay together and decide to join up with one of my enemies, they would pose more of a threat than I want to face. What I must do is separate them—use them as far as I can, then make sure they don't get together again."

Aloud he said, "You're used to working as a team, I suppose?"

"Yes, Your Majesty," said Castor. "We fight as a unit."

"But I have separate tasks," said Peleus. "Both urgent, but one more difficult than the other. Working singly, you will earn double fees, and be able to rejoin each other in a few days."

"Tell us more," said Pollux.

"To the northwest," said the king, "lies the island of Bebrycos. It is ruled by a monster named Amycus, a giant who butts people to death. No one has survived a visit to that place. Everyone who lands there has to fight Amycus or is cut down on the spot. It is said that the dented skulls of those who fought him form a tower higher than his castle. For years now I have been

*The king, for all his girth, has no softness about him.*

45

offering a rich reward to anyone who could vanquish Amycus. Many have tried, but no one has claimed the reward."

"What is the other task?" asked Castor.

"Tricky . . . difficult . . . but much less dangerous. On a small round island, about twenty miles to the east, dwells an evil young magician."

"What makes him so magical?" asked Pollux.

"He holds unholy sway over the birds and beasts of that place," said Peleus. "Wolves and bears attend him. Snakes dance to his fluting. All foul wizardry, of course, and should be stamped out. Besides, he pretends to be my cousin, the son of the late king, and actually dares to claim my throne."

"How is it you haven't been able to kill him long before this?" asked Castor.

"I can't send ships against him. That island is surrounded by a hidden reef that tears the bottom out of any vessel. But a strong swimmer can cross over unharmed. I'd like one of you to go there, strangle the tricky little rat, whose name is Jason, by the way, and return with some proof of his death. His head, perhaps, but any reasonable proof will do. That is the second task. It should take only a day or so, then he who has done it will be able to join his brother on Bebrycos."

The twins looked at each other, nodded simultaneously to the king, and walked out of the throne room. As they left the castle, Castor said:

"It's my turn for the dangerous task."

"How do you figure?"

"You're the one who took on the shark."

"Only because you were busy tying knots in the octopus," said Pollux. "But we won't quarrel. You can go to Bebrycos first. I'm curious to see what that young animal tamer looks like."

"I'll tell you," said Castor. "I'm uneasy about things. I don't trust Peleus."

"I'd be worried about you if you did," said Pollux. "He's

a putrid lump of lard, every ounce of him. But I don't think he'll move against us as long as he believes we're doing things for him. And he pays very well."

"I'm still uneasy," said Castor. "Let's do the stump-water thing."

This was a homely magic shared by the twins since they were small boys. What they did was go into the woods and find a tree stump in which rainwater had collected. They stood on opposite sides of the stump, inhaling its special smell of water and decayed wood and steeping leaves, all the while gazing into the puddle. They would go into a light trance and see pictures in the water. When they came out of the trance they would tell each other what they had seen. More often than not they had seen exactly the same things. If so, they believed, the matched images were telling what would happen to them in the near future.

*They stood on opposite sides of the stump, inhaling its special smell of water and decayed wood and steeping leaves, all the while gazing into the puddle.*

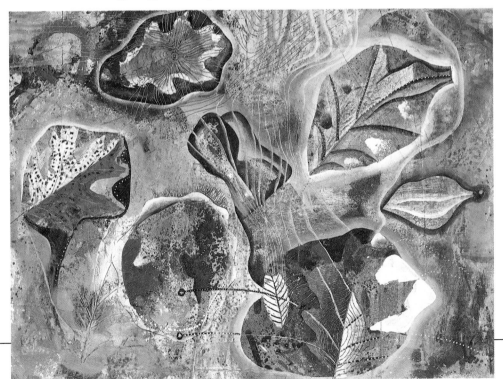

But these visions were not always reliable. Sometimes the pictures came true, other times not, and often led the twins into dangerous error. But they had happy natures. They remembered only what had come true and forgot what hadn't. And, when in doubt about anything, still consulted the stump water.

Now, they went into the woods and found a stump. They stood on opposite sides of it and leaned over, taking deep breaths. It was bright afternoon but the stump was enveloped in its own time—neither day nor night, but a kind of livid twilight. A cheesy moon hung low, and the face in the moon was the face of Peleus, leering at them.

A ship, tiny as a twig, perfectly made, graceful as a gull, scudded across the puddle, sails full. On the deck were minute figures whom the twins recognized as themselves. In the bow stood a black-haired, slender lad, very young, but obviously in command.

A fog blew over the stump, almost hiding the ship. As the twins watched, the thick mist wreathed into pictures. Giants, slavering ogres, witches with tangled hair and bloody claws. And, in a place they had never been, an altar covered by a strangely colored fleece, purple and gold, the colors shifting and mixing as in a dawn sky . . . then, sliding into the scene, an enormous serpent, jaws agape.

The fog blew away, taking the ship with it, and dissolving their trance. The twins found themselves staring into an ordinary stump that held a puddle of rainwater. They looked at each other.

"What did you see?" asked Castor.

Pollux told him about the ship, its crew, the wreathing shapes, and the moon face of Peleus leering over all. "That's what I saw," said Pollux. "What about you?"

"Exactly the same, every detail."

"Well, the old stump-water magic is still working," said Pollux. "How do you read it?"

"We're destined to take a voyage, obviously. Meet giants,

48

ogres, witches, serpents, and all the things that moved in the fog."

"Yes," said Pollux. "How about that skipper, did you recognize him?"

"No. And he looked mighty young and puny to be leading us. One thing I know is true; I thought so before, but now I'm sure. We can't trust Peleus. Want he wants is for us to do some dirty work for him and get ourselves killed doing it. And I think it's Amycus who's supposed to do the killing."

"So I'll finish off my job as soon as possible, and join you on Bebrycos."

"Well, I hope I won't need too much help," said Castor. "But if I do, I'll wait for you."

The twins embraced briefly, and parted.

# 8

# Jason, the Healer

s the king had said, some miles off the coast of Iolcus lay the little round island where Jason dwelt. He was the only person there, but didn't realize how lonesome he was because he had many animal friends.

Nevertheless, he sometimes felt that he would like to meet someone more like himself, and would spend hours standing on the beach gazing at the dim bulk of the mainland. He was especially excited when he saw a ship sailing toward him. Sometimes one would come close enough for him to see tiny figures moving on the deck, but always a ship would come only so near, then sheer off abruptly—and the lad would wonder why. He had no way of knowing that Poseidon had girded the island with a hidden reef.

But for some time now he had been too busy to watch for ships. He was trying to solve an important problem. For among the many snakes on this island was one that was particularly vicious—a small green viper, unbelievably swift, whose bite sent animals into foaming fits. The poison didn't actually kill them, but, maddened by pain, they would often shatter their skull against rocks or trees, or claw themselves to pieces. Now, Jason had taught himself to cure ordinary snakebites, even ones that were quite deadly, but he wasn't able to approach an animal bitten by the viper, for, in its madness, it would have killed him. He had to stand by and watch it destroy itself. He knew that if he could only quiet these viper-bitten animals, somehow, he would be able to draw out the venom, but he didn't know how to quiet them. And he kept thinking about how to do it.

He had been studying the flight of bees because he liked to eat honeycombs. Bees astounded him. They flew so fast, so hard—like flung stones—but they could also hover, float, change direction; they seemed the most active of all creatures. But he noticed that after visiting a certain flower bed, the bees would slow up considerably, wobble in flight, seem almost to drowse as they flew.

He examined these flowers. They were unfamiliar. He thought that he knew every kind of flower that grew on the island, but these seemed to have sprouted overnight. Black and purple blossoms, except for a single flame-colored petal. He tore off a leaf and ate it. And immediately felt himself sinking into sleep.

Dreams thronged. He saw a young god, Morpheus, standing in the dark chamber of his father, Hypnos, God of Sleep. "I am weary, my son," said Hypnos. "You must help me tonight. You must fly about the world distributing my gift."

"Very well," said Morpheus, "but I wish to mix my own colors of sleep. Yours are too dark and thick and sad."

"So it has been and so it must be," said Hypnos. "For it is a little trial death we put upon man each night to prepare him for the long final death."

Morpheus, dissatisfied, went to his cousin, Persephone, the flower princess, and said: "Help me, sweet maiden, you who go with your paint box among the flowers each spring. I do not wish to scatter little deaths but hours of repose. I need something to brighten sleep."

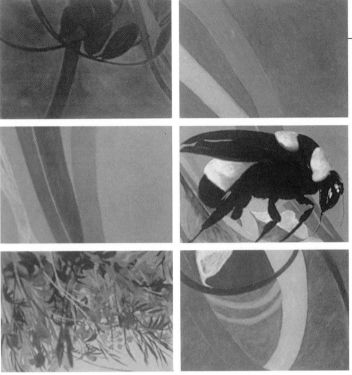

*Jason noticed that after visiting
a certain flower bed, the bees
would slow up considerably.*

"Yes," said Persephone. "Sleep can be brightened by something called *dreams*. Humankind is ready for them now. Take this."

She moved her slender hand through the air. In her fingers a flower blossomed. She gave it to Morpheus. "See, Cousin, black and purple like sleep with one fire-red petal for dreams. We shall call it the *lotus*. Plant it first in Libya where it is always summer; it will do well there. But save a cutting for a certain small island in the Middle Sea, where someone will someday use it in a very timely way."

When Jason awoke, he knew what to do. He gathered an armful of blossoms, which grew thicker than ever, and took them to his hut. He chopped up the petals, mixed them with pure springwater, and boiled the brew until it was thick and gummy. Then dipped his arrowheads in it.

He took bow and arrows and prowled the woods until he heard a bugling, a clattering. He followed the sound into a clearing where two stags were fighting. Horns locked, heaving; they were writhing shapes of brute strength. He notched an arrow, drew his bow, and loosed the shaft, aiming so that he would just nick the haunch of one stag. The arrow sang through the air, flying true. The stag immediately collapsed. The other one stood over him, eyes rolling in astonishment. Jason ran to the fallen stag, which was breathing evenly, unhurt, but fast asleep.

Jason whooped with joy. In his exultance, he leaped upon the other stag and rode it out of the woods onto the beach. He galloped along the beach, shouting with joy. A black goat and blue fox raced after him. He saw something white coasting in on a wave. It landed on the beach and sat there in his path. He stopped the stag in mid-stride and looked down at a snow-white seal. The whiskered face gazing up at him looked so clever that he almost expected to hear words coming from its mouth. Nevertheless, he was astonished when the seal did speak.

"Do you know who you are?" asked the seal.

"I'm me," said Jason.

"Is that all you know about yourself?"

"What else is there to know?"

"Much . . . much . . . Do you remember how you came here?"

*"We shall call it the* lotus.*"*

"I've tried to forget."

"Can you?"

"I don't want to talk about it."

"Then I will," said the seal. "You were asleep in your nursery. Dreadful sounds awoke you. Men shouting, women screaming. Torches flared. You remember your nurse's hand snatching you out of bed and wrapping you in a cloak. She is running with you; you hear her feet on the marble floor. Outside now, cold air, gull cries, sea smells, the hiss of the surf. You are in the small boat in your nurse's lap. You hear oars dipping. You are rocked to sleep. You awake upon this island. Then day follows day in a bright blur. You are a little boy living alone except for animals. A she-goat and a blue fox. You drink milk from the goat; the fox brings you nuts and berries and honeycombs, until you learn to gather them for yourself and to take fish from the sea."

"You seem to know all about me," said Jason.

"Yes. I have watched over you since that dreadful night."

"Who are you?"

"I am he who serves his master. My name is Proteus."

"Who's your master?"

"Poseidon, God of the Sea."

"Is it he who bids you watch over me?"

"It is he."

"What is his interest in me?"

"You shall know presently. First, let me unravel that terrible scene. The shouts were your father, the king, being murdered by his cousin, Peleus, who wished to be king himself. After killing your father he was coming to kill you, the heir to the throne. But your nurse, a remarkable woman, fled the castle with you in her arms, found a boatman and hired his boat. My master then, who had been observing all this, spoke from the sea, guiding her to this island and bidding her leave you here. She knew it was a god speaking and obeyed, although it broke her heart to

*Jason took bow and arrows and prowled the woods*
*until he heard a bugling, a clattering.*
*He followed the sound.*

abandon you. Then I was ordered to arrange for your care. I instructed the goat and the fox, and in various forms have visited this island from time to time to see how you fared."

"And why do you reveal yourself to me now?" asked Jason. "What has changed?"

"You have. You have grown. Growth is slow change. You are old enough now."

"Old enough for what?"

"To know," said the seal. "Then to do."

"Do what?"

"Act upon your knowledge. I have informed you that you are the rightful king."

"King of what?"

"That fair land called Iolcus, which you can dimly see from this shore."

"Have you come to tell me that I must claim my kingdom?"

"Hearken now. Your cousin Peleus, your enemy, is a famed battle chief. His army has swept over frontiers, subduing neighbors and adding their lands to his. His war fleet raids island kingdoms. Before you can even think of confronting him, you must learn to fight, learn to lead."

"How do I begin?"

"You have begun."

"What is my first task?"

"To survive another day."

"I seem to have lasted this long. Why is one more day so important?"

"Because someone is coming to kill you. The king knows where you are and has sent an assassin—who is to wring your neck like a chicken, then twist your head off and bring it to Peleus to prove that you are dead."

"What's he like, this assassin?"

"Extremely beautiful, and even more deadly. One of a pair of twins, Spartan princes, so tall and strong and handsome it is as if whoever made the eldest took one look and immediately decided that there had to be another of his kind."

"Are they both coming after me?"

"Just one. That's all I can tell you. Take care."

The seal slid into the sea and vanished.

# 9

# The Assassin

ears do not howl. They rumble, they snarl, they chuckle; when in pain they utter a kind of sobbing roar. And it was this agonized roaring that awakened Jason just before dawn. He snatched up bow and arrows and rushed toward the sound. He knew it must be a bear, bitten by a viper, and clawing itself in a foaming fit. He sped through the wood into a clearing, and saw not one bear but two, a brown one and a black one, both huge, both maddened by pain and foaming at the mouth, and trying to tear each other to pieces before turning on themselves.

They were a whirling, furry mass. Jason notched an arrow, but hesitated. He was afraid that if he put one to sleep, the other would kill it before he could shoot a second arrow. He hesitated too long; the black bear flung the brown one halfway across the clearing. It landed next to Jason and swung its paw, knocking the bow from his hands.

He sprawled on the ground, groping for his bow. But the beast was upon him. Hot, meaty breath gusted against his face, choking him. He felt claws of fire raking his shoulder, then a coolness of blood. He knew he was about to feel a final crunching pain as the bear crushed his head between its jaws.

Swooning, he was dazzled by gold. Weight was lifted from him. "I'm dead," he thought. "This is the inlaid floor of heaven. Why was I not taken to Tartarus? Or is hell paved with gold also?"

When his vision cleared he saw a tall, yellow-haired youth fighting the brown bear. The beast stood erect, clawing at the youth—who was punching so fast that his fists were one streak of motion. Jason heard the bear's rib cage crack. The animal fell, spitting blood, then lay still. But the victorious youth was suddenly encircled by two enormous furry arms as the black bear attacked from behind, taking him into a hug that was certain death.

Jason had scooped up his bow. He notched an arrow now, and knowing how difficult it was for him to hit the bear without grazing the youth, thought a swift prayer. "Poseidon, guide my arrow!" And let fly. The shaft whizzed past the youth's head, passing so close that its feathers brushed the yellow hair before burying itself in the bear's shoulder. The furry arms loosened; the bear fell.

Instantaneously, the youth whirled, drawing a knife, and kneeling. Jason, astounded, saw that the stranger, absolutely unruffled by killing one beast and almost being killed by the other, was preparing to skin the black bear.

"Don't!" shouted Jason.

The youth swiveled his head. Jason saw that his eyes were not blue but gray, glinting now like frost. "Don't what?" he said. "I want its hide."

"No."

"Why not?"

"It isn't dead. It's asleep."

"Looks dead."

"It's not. My arrows are dipped in sleep."

*Jason saw a tall, yellow-haired youth*
*fighting the brown bear . . . and heard*
*the bear's rib cage crack.*

"Well, I know mine is dead. I hit it square. So I'll just cut this one's throat and skin 'em both. Make a couple of bearskin cloaks for my brother and me. It gets cold in Sparta."

"Are you Spartan?"

"I am. Pollux is my name."

"Are you a prince by any chance?"

Pollux nodded.

"A twin?"

"All three."

"Then you've come to kill me, haven't you?"

"Are you Jason?"

"Yes."

"Whatever I've come to do, I can't. You saved my life."

"You saved mine first."

"Well, we saved each other. Killing you is out of the question, worse luck. I was promised a fat fee." Jason saw the prince cocking his golden head and staring down at him, studying his face intently.

"Why are you looking at me like that?"

"Do something for me. Wash the dirt and blood off."

Jason went to a stream, dipped his head in, and swabbed his face with a handful of dry grass. He came back to the Spartan.

"Yes . . ." said Pollux. "It grows more and more curious."

"What does?"

"You're the lad we saw in the stump water, my twin and I. We are to go voyaging with you. We shared a vision at the stump and saw you captaining a ship that was sailing toward strange encounters."

"I don't know what all that means, but it sounds marvelous."

"Are you saying you don't know anything about an expedition you're supposed to lead? How can that be?"

"I *was* told that if I survived your visit I would be seeking adventure to train me for kingship."

"Who told you?"

"A seal."

"Do you usually hold conversations with seals?"

"This one serves Poseidon. Why do you look so doubtful? Talking seals are as believable as stump-water visions."

"Well, I can tell you what your first adventure will be. We're going to Bebrycos, you and I, to help my brother fight a brass-headed giant."

"Oh joy! I haven't done much fighting, but I'm a pretty good archer."

"We'll teach you whatever you need to know," said Pollux.

*"I haven't done much fighting,*
*but I'm a pretty good archer."*

"You're our little brother now." He drew Jason to him and pressed his bleeding knuckles to the boy's clawed shoulder. "Our blood has mingled," he said. "We're brothers. Which means you're Castor's brother, too."

"I couldn't ask for anything better."

"Gather your sleepy arrows, Little Brother. Fill your quiver. We're off to Bebrycos at the turning of the tide!"

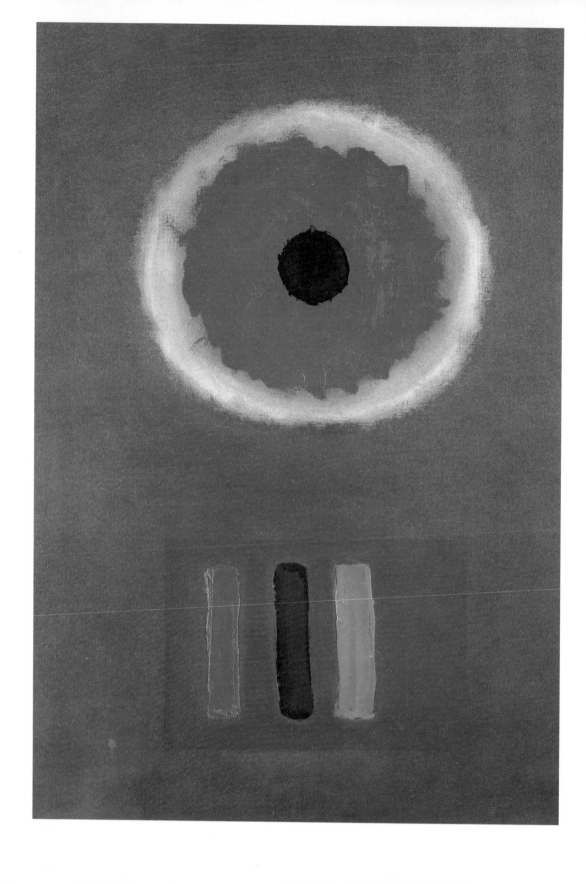

# 10

# The Scorching

**W**hen Castor landed on Bebrycos he spent a few days scouting the island before challenging its ruler. His only knowledge of the giant and of those he ruled was what Peleus had told him, and he decided to see for himself what the situation was.

He pretended to be an old crippled man, a beggar. Donning a ragged black cloak, he stooped to half his height, hid his face in the cowl, and went limping about the island, occasionally thrusting a bowl at people, begging for food in a high quavering voice.

He learned that Amycus ruled by terror, that even his courtiers were not safe because he would be taken by gusts of rage, seize the nearest person, and pound him to a pulp. Only the Royal Guard, who were the twenty wingless dragons, was safe from his furies. He would kill anyone who displeased him. Some offenders were chained to a rock at a low tide and would spend hours waiting for the rising tide to cover them. But since sharks prowled very close to shore, only the lucky ones drowned.

A prime offender, anyone who dared look too long at any

girl Amycus was interested in, was given to the guard for special treatment. The dragons would take the man to the beach, shackle him to a massive iron ring sunk into an enormous charred boulder, and stand in a circle blowing flame at him, one dragon at a time—roasting him inch by inch until his screams were heard in the castle, making Amycus smile. Some victims tried to shorten their agony by beating their head against the rock, but only a few had wit enough to do that.

These torture sessions drew big crowds, and the old beggar sidled among them, unnoticed, observing everything. He felt an idea forming. He tried to fend it off, because it was unspeakably perilous, but the idea kept coming back, and he knew he would have to think it through.

Upon this day, the spectators were disappointed. The man being burned was inconsiderate enough to die quickly. The crowd drifted away. The old beggar stayed on the beach watching the gulls. Attracted by the smell of burned flesh, they were diving, screeching, waiting for the body to cool so that they could feast. In the meantime, they ate the big black crabs that had also come to dine. It was an unpleasant sight, but Castor had come to do something, and had to stay until it was done.

He waited until the bones were stripped clean and the gulls had departed. He went to the rock, took hold of the iron ring, braced his legs, and began to pull. The rock seemed as though it were rooted to the center of the earth; he could not budge it. He exerted all his strength—which, he realized now, he had never really used to its fullest. "Things have been too easy for me," he said to himself. "Nothing I've ever wrestled, man or beast, has lasted two minutes against me. Now, let's see what I'm really made of." He pulled with all his might, and more than his might. Every particle of him fused into a wild surge of energy.

He thought he felt the rock move. "Father Zeus, help me," he muttered. The gigantic rock seemed to loosen in its socket of earth. He grunted and let go. "If I can do this much now," he

*The dragons would . . .
stand in a circle
blowing flame.*

thought, "a few licks of fire should really inspire me."

He wandered off then. He felt dizzy from the strain, but had done enough to know that he could do more. He left that place, for the smell of burned flesh still hung heavy, and walked a mile or so along the shore, thinking hard.

"It's definite then," he said to himself. "I've got to do it and try to get it done before Pollux comes . . . which means he'll be the one to challenge Amycus. Because even if I succeed against the dragons—which is a very big *if* indeed—I'll probably be too scorched to fight the giant. I wish we could trade jobs, Pollux and I, but he doesn't have the temperament to handle the dragons. When faced by an enemy he lowers his head and charges. He hates tactics and trickery; he trusts only his fists. But these damned lizards must be taken care of or neither of us will get out of here alive, no matter what happens to Amycus. As for those slithering flamethrowers, there's only one thing to do, and only me to do it."

He had come now to where he had hidden his own clothes.

He stripped himself of the stinking beggar rags and plunged into the sea, and swam until he felt clean again. Then he donned his tunic and went to find the girl he had seen with Amycus.

He went to the castle grounds and lurked in the orchard, watching the great portal until he saw the girl come out. He waited again until he saw three dragons emerge from the castle, one of them carrying a big net. This was the girl's escort, he knew, assigned by Amycus to follow her and discourage any other suitors. They followed very slowly.

Castor hurried after her with long strides. He wanted some time alone with her before the dragons arrived. He followed her up a hill. Looking back, he saw that the dragons were far behind. He guessed that they were giving her plenty of space, hoping that she was really going to meet someone. Then they could catch him, and begin the scorching. They enjoyed their work.

When he reached her she was sitting on a rock, sobbing.

"What's the matter?" he asked.

She choked back her sobs and looked at him. Her wet face was very beautiful.

"Why are you crying?"

"It's that beast, the king, my brother-in-law. He's tired of my sister and wants to marry me."

"I take it that doesn't appeal to you?"

"Oh no, sir. I hate, loathe and despise him."

"How about your sister?"

"She has nothing to say about it. When he gets tired of a wife he throws her away and gets a new one. My sister's his eighth."

"And you'll be the ninth?"

"And my little sister will probably be the tenth. He'll be ready to throw me away when she's big enough. But I won't be the ninth, I won't marry him, I won't! I came here to jump off this hill."

"Don't do that," said Castor. "You're too beautiful. It

would be too much of a waste. There must be many young men who love you."

"There was one I loved, but he's gone. The king's lizards caught him in a net and did dreadful things to him. You'd better go away, sir, or they'll catch you, too. They follow me everywhere."

Castor saw her eyes widen in terror, and knew that she saw dragons coming up behind him. He stepped closer, whispering, "May I kiss you?" And felt the net fall over him.

He didn't resist as the three dragons dragged him to the beach. He drew deep into himself as he had trained himself to do before a fight. He let all anxiety drain away, and tried to draw upon all the sources of his strength, some of which were mysterious even to himself.

He let them take him to the rock and chain him to its iron ring. He saw the crowd gather, watched the gulls thronging above in preparation for their feast. He made himself be absolutely passive because he wanted all the dragons to form their close circle around him. And he wanted them to be without suspicion.

When the green monsters closed their circle about the rock, one of them opened crocodile jaws and spat flame. A narrow jet. Castor braced his legs and began to pull, trying to lift the rock. It did not budge. He strained harder. His tunic had burned away and the crowd saw his back muscles writhing like serpents. Another dragon spat flame, then another.

Castor was prepared for pain, but he had been unable to imagine this kind of agony. "Father Zeus," he groaned. "Help me—please . . ."

Another dragon shot flame, aiming at his middle.

Castor smelled flesh burning—his own, he knew—and the odor of it filled him with fury such as he had never known. Fury became strength. The crowd saw him sink toward the ground, then arise mightily, pulling the enormous rock out of the earth as a cork is drawn from a bottle. Astounded, they watched him pivot, swinging the boulder at the end of his chain. Saw him spin, faster and faster, and the tethered rock whirled in a murderous circuit, crushing dragons as it went.

No one had ever heard the giant lizards make a sound before. But now they were howling, a rattling phlegmy screech as they fell before the rock. As they fell, however, they belched final fire at Castor, great gouts of it now until he was bathed in fire.

But he kept whirling until all the dragons had fallen. Then he collapsed, falling among them, sprawling on the sand. The crowd had fled in terror. The green bodies lay still. Only the golden one writhed slightly. Castor, in agony, lay there praying for death to stop his pain.

And that is how Jason and Pollux found him, lying on the

*Castor, in agony, lay there praying for death to stop his pain.*

sand among the broken lizards. Pollux gasped in horror. "What are these ghastly things?" he whispered.

"Whatever they are," said Jason, "he seems to have killed them all."

"But they've killed him, too," sobbed Pollux.

Jason was kneeling at Castor's side, touching him gently. "He's still alive," he said.

"Look at him, though," cried Pollux. "Half his skin's burned off. He's in awful pain. I'm going to put him out of his misery, then follow him to Tartarus. We have two bodies but a single soul. I can't live without my twin."

Jason felt himself melting with pity, but he tried not to show it. He knew he had to imitate coolness. "Do you really want to die before avenging him?" he said. "Don't you want to fight Amycus first? You owe it to your brother who has prepared the way. Besides, the giant might spare you the trouble of killing yourself."

"I know," groaned Pollux. "I want to fight him. But how can I leave Castor in this pain?"

"I can do something," said Jason. He drew an arrow from his quiver and scratched Castor's forehead. The moaning immediately ceased, and the writhing. Castor breathed easily. "He's asleep," said Jason. "He feels no pain. He'll gain strength as he sleeps. When he awakes, I'll heal his burns. I promise."

Pollux knelt and kissed his brother's face. Then grasped Jason and cried, "Let's find Amycus then! I must fight! I can't wait!"

He rushed off and Jason followed.

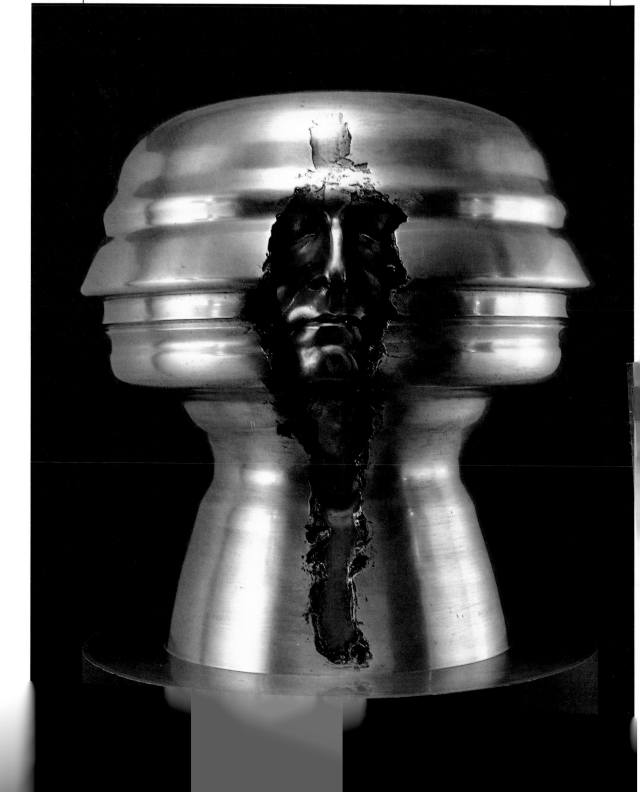

# 11

# Hero Meets Monster

By the time they reached the castle, word had already come to Amycus that his dragons had been battered to death. The news sent him into one of his rages, and he had killed three of his courtiers and was holding a fourth by the neck, strangling him, while issuing orders to the captain of his spearmen.

"They say it was a stranger who killed my dragons. A big blond youth, a Spartan. Find him, and bring him to me; I want to kill him with my own hands. Very slowly, and so painfully that he'll wish he had let the dragons burn him."

"I'm a Spartan," called a voice. "Will I do?"

Amycus gaped in astonishment as he saw Pollux and Jason standing in front of his throne.

"Yes, I'm a Spartan," said Pollux. "And blond. Not big by your standards, you overgrown brute, but big enough to make things interesting if you dare fight me."

The king was speechless, and everyone knew he was too furious to utter a word. Jason was watching him closely. The brass head could not change expression, but Jason, who had trained himself to observe body changes, saw the veins swell in the giant's neck. Saw the thick brown pelt that covered his torso grow spiky, like the hackles of an angered wolf. But when Amycus did speak, it was in a whisper, and somehow more menacing than if he had bellowed.

"Are you he who killed my dragons?"

"Not me," said Pollux. "But someone very much like me. My twin, in fact. He has lost too much skin to do any fighting this week, so if you're really itching to avenge yourself on anyone, I suggest myself. How many times do I have to challenge you, you bowl-headed monstrosity? Let's go out to your blood-soaked meadow and fight."

"Can you be ready by midafternoon?" said Amycus.

"I'm ready now."

"I need a few hours to send word out so that we may have a good audience. I want as many people as possible there to see what I do to you."

"Midafternoon, then," said Pollux.

Jason had been studying the giant all this while, and was dismayed at what he saw. Although he respected his friend's skill, he didn't see how he could possibly stand up to a creature as powerful as the king. Amycus was about ten feet tall. His burnished brass head with its flat nose and ridged eye holes was simply a mallet. His neck was long and very thick, as wide as his head—one length of muscle, giving that murderous whiplike power to his butting. His shoulders were as wide as an ox yoke, his legs like tree trunks; his arms were almost as long as his legs. And although Jason could not see muscle under the bearlike pelt, he knew it was there. His hands were as big as garden spades. When clenched, they would be knobs of bone almost as hard as his head.

Jason cast a sidelong glance at Pollux, who was also staring at the king and was utterly undismayed at what he saw. A little smile played over his lips. His gray eyes were pale as frost.

"Go to the meadow now," said the king, "and examine the ground. I want you to have every chance to make a fight of it."

"Thank you, Your Majesty," said Pollux. "I don't think you'll be disappointed in my efforts."

He walked out of the throne room, the courtiers parting before him. Jason followed.

Jason was restless, seething with anxiety. He strolled about as Pollux studied the meadow. The hillside was filling with people. They were seating themselves on boulders along the slopes. A vast throng was gathering. Jason crossed to where Pollux was standing. "Have you chosen your ground?" he asked.

"Here," said Pollux. It was a spot where the field tapered toward a cliff face, a wall of sheer rock.

"Why here?" asked Jason. "Wouldn't you do better in the middle of the field where your speed would count? He'll simply corner you here and pound you to pieces."

"Exactly what I want him to think," said Pollux.

Jason stayed with him now, waiting for the king to come. People were mobbing the slopes; it looked as though the entire population of the island had come. Vendors passed among them, selling prawns, honeycombs, and melons.

The king strode onto the meadow, surrounded by spearmen, attended by slaves. He went directly to Pollux. "Are you prepared to die?" he growled.

"I'm prepared to fight."

"Have you chosen your ground?"

"Here," said Pollux. "This rock wall is one boundary. The dimensions are whatever you choose."

The king turned to his spearmen. "Pace it off. Fifteen strides long, fifteen strides wide. Stand your pickets."

An officer paced off the distance and placed the men along the boundaries, making a square with the wall at one end. The armored men were a hedge of iron.

A trumpeter raised his horn and blew a clear blast. Then he addressed the crowd. "People of Bebrycos, you are gathered here to watch your king, Amycus, protector of the realm and hammer of justice, punish one who dares enter our land without invitation. Watch the fellow perish. Watch and admire."

As this was being announced, the king's slaves were strip-

*A vast throng was gathering.*

ping their master. The sun glinted on his brass head. The trumpeter sounded his horn again. The fight began.

Pollux was a big youth, but he looked very small as he backed away from the stalking giant. Jason watched in anguish as the king worked every advantage of the tightly penned space. He could corner Pollux here, maul him with his great fists until he was ready for the death butt. Yet Pollux himself had chosen this place. Jason couldn't understand why.

But it was strange what was happening in the ring. It seemed more like a dance than a fight. Amycus shuffled after the youth, blocking him with shoulders and elbows, swinging at him. But Pollux drifted away from those fists and from those massive furry arms—moving very thriftily, just enough to escape the flailing fists. Stepping lightly away from the bull-like charges, dancing, twirling, dodging. He was untouched, though Amycus had aimed a hundred blows at him. He was untouched, but had not yet struck a blow of his own.

Suddenly, Pollux changed tactics. He stopped dancing and began to leap. He sprang from one side of the ring to the other.

As soon as he touched ground he leaped again. Amycus rushed after him. Just as he reached him, Pollux rose straight into the air. He leaped higher than the king's head and launched a scything sideways kick. Amycus ducked, and the foot whizzed past his head. Jason thought, "Why does he duck? Kicking that head is kicking brass. The foot must break."

Amycus must have thought the same thing at the same time. For, as Pollux landed with knees bent and immediately sprang into the air again and kicked again, this time the king did not duck. But foot did not meet head. It was exquisitely aimed. As Pollux came down, his foot swerved in the air and sank into the king's torso. He bent over, gasping.

But Amycus straightened up, immediately seeming to gain new strength from the pain. He bellowed, charged again. Pollux sprang away. This time Amycus did not rush after him but dove through the air. Dove halfway across the ring, hitting Pollux with his shoulder and hurling him against the hedge of armored men—who pushed him back into the ring.

Amycus was all over him now, blocking escape, mauling

him. A terrific punch caught Pollux between shoulder and elbow. His left arm went limp. His mouth bled. The crowd roared. But it seemed that the taste of his own blood refreshed the Spartan. He moved swiftly, stepping away from Amycus, twirling, dancing, springing away, swaying out of reach. As reeds sway before a wind, so Pollux bent away from the giant's flailing fists.

Amycus was breathing heavily now. He kept rushing, punching. Now Pollux began to strike back, using only his right arm. He did not aim at the brass face, but at the body. The king's rib cage boomed like a drum under the youth's lightning fist. Nine blows Pollux struck, and whisked away before Amycus could strike back. The king's massive body was hidden by his pelt; it was hard to tell the effect of these blows. But Jason judged his torso to be one big bruise.

The giant's strength was undiminished, however—or so it seemed. He plowed ahead now, accepting all the punishment Pollux offered, taking all his punches, trying to get close enough

*A trumpeter raised his horn*
*and blew a clear blast.*

to use his mallet head. The tactic filled Jason with anguish as he watched. It seemed to be working. Pollux was retreating, but straight back, without springing away. Jason thought he might be too tired to leap.

Amycus shuffled toward him, like a bear moving toward a fawn. Pollux retreated until he was stopped by the wall. He slumped against the rock, and Amycus was where he wanted to be. He did not punch, but seized the youth's shoulders, and drew back his head for the fatal butt. And in Jason's vision, the presence of death thickened the air, slowing everything. He saw the brass head smashing through the sunlight toward that beautiful face.

Then, more swiftly than the eye could follow, the yellow head twitched away. It moved just enough so that the king's head barely grazed it, and smashed into the rock wall. The roaring of the crowd changed into a vast sigh as it saw the rock wall split. Fracture lines radiated from the dent. And for a moment, it seemed, the brass head was socketed in the rock, holding Amycus still. Only a moment, but enough for Pollux to slip away behind him, and to raise his own fist.

He pivoted on the soles of his feet and smashed his bleeding knuckles into the brown pelt, just above the waist—a terrible kidney punch that would have killed anyone else. But Amycus turned to face his foe. The brass forehead was dented slightly, his face was scratched, but he seemed otherwise unhurt. When he moved, however, he moved slowly; something was muffling him. He lifted his arms—slowly. Pollux's left hand clawed itself painfully into the air; the arm was indeed broken. With two fingers of his left hand he lifted the king's chin in what looked like a weird caress.

He swung his right fist again. He planted his feet, turned on his ankles and twisted his body around with all the whiplike power of his spine, all the elastic strength of his shoulders, all his love of fighting, and all his loathing of the brass-headed brute who had caused his brother such agony.

*The rock wall split.*
*Fracture lines radiated*
*from the dent.*

His fist landed on the giant's throat. Jason, watching breathlessly, felt that he was attached to that fist, and he could feel the king's windpipe breaking under the blow. Amycus swayed on the grass. Blood gushed from every hole in the metal face. From nostrils, ears, mouth. He bellowed weakly, blowing bubbles of blood—then fell face down. And everyone in the vast crowd knew he would not rise again.

The people were yelling, jumping, screeching, roaring—not with rage but with joy. For now that Amycus was dead they could show what they felt. Jason rushed to Pollux and threw his arms about him.

"Want to be king?" he whispered. "They'll sit you right on the throne, if you wish."

"I don't know," said Pollux. "I'd have to talk it over with Castor. He'd have to share the throne, you know."

"No!" called a voice.

The young men turned. It was a seal rearing up on the bright grass, flipper raised. "No," he repeated. "My master, Poseidon, has other plans. You must go voyaging, the three of you, but in a proper ship this time. And other heroes will join the crew. From island to island you shall sail, seeking a magical prize, rescuing maidens as you go, killing monsters, cleansing my master's sea. Then, Jason, you will be ready for kingship, and all of you shall enter legend."

"Spooky stuff," murmured Pollux, grinning. "Let's go find Castor. He'll be waiting to hear about the fight."

"A master builder shall come," called the seal. "He'll build you a ship. Wait for him here."

And the seal slid into the sea.

# Acknowledgments

Letter Cap Illustrations by Hrana L. Janto

Cover, AMYCUS *(1988) by Maria Ruotolo (37" × 48")*
   Courtesy of the artist
      Photo: Karen Bell

Opposite page 1, NEPTUNE COMMANDING THE SEA *(1982) by Earl Staley, acrylic on canvas (62 1/2" × 47")*
   Courtesy of the artist

Page 2, *Detail from* WISDOM VICTORIOUS OVER VICES *by Andrea Mantegna (1431–1506), oil on canvas*
   Courtesy of the Louvre, Paris
      Photo: Art Resource, NY

Page 4, *Detail from* THE ERUPTION OF VESUVIUS *by Jean Baptiste Genillon (1750–1829), oil on canvas*
   Courtesy of La Museé des Beaux Arts, Lille
      Photo: Giraudon/Art Resource, NY

Page 9, *Detail from* THE MONTH OF SEPTEMBER, THE TRIUMPH OF VULCAN *by Cossa Cossi (1435–77), fresco*
   Courtesy of Palazzo di Schifanoia, Ferrara
      Photo: Scala/Art Resource, NY

Page 11, ACIS AND GALATEA *by F. Perrier (ca. 1584–1650), oil on canvas*
   Courtesy of the Louvre, Paris
      Photo: Art Resource, NY

Page 12, *Detail from* THE PALACE OF AMSTERDAM WITH EXOTIC BIRDS *by Melchior d'Hondecoeter (1636–95), oil on canvas*
   Courtesy of Roy Miles Fine Paintings, London
      Photo: Bridgeman/Art Resource, NY

Page 14, *Central detail from* THE THREE TREES *by Ralph Blakelock (1847–1919), oil on canvas*
   Courtesy of the Hirshhorn Museum & Sculpture Garden, Smithsonian Institution, Washington, D.C.
      Photo: Joseph Martin/Scala/Art Resource, NY

Page 16, SEA LION, *an illustration from* FAUNA JAPONICA SIVE DESCRIPTIO ANIMALIUM *(1850)*
   Courtesy of the Department of Library Services, American Museum of Natural History, NY (K14291)

Page 18, BAPTISMAL SCENE *(1945) by Mark Rothko (1903–70), watercolor on paper (19 7/8" × 14")*

Courtesy of Collection of the Whitney Museum of American Art, NY. Purchase 46.12

Page 21, LA NYMPHE DE LA SEINE *by Jean Goujon (1510–68), bas relief*
    Courtesy of the Louvre, Paris
        Photo: Giraudon/Art Resource, NY

Page 22, LA POLYPE DEFORME FLOTTAIT SUR LE RIVAGE *by Odilon Redon (1840–1916), etching*
    Courtesy of Bibliothèque Nationale, Paris

Page 24, *Detail from* MASK-FIGURE, *Bakota, French Equatorial Africa*
    Courtesy of the Department of Library Services, American Museum of Natural History, NY (K9909)
        Photo: Philip Gifford

Page 27, MARINE FAUNA *(ca. 1st century), Roman mosaic*
    Courtesy of the National Museum, Naples
        Photo: Scala/Art Resource, NY

Page 30, FIGURE ON A TIGHTROPE *by William Baziotes (1912–63), oil on canvas (36" × 42")*
    Courtesy of the Metropolitan Museum of Art, Gift of Dr. and Mrs. Louis R. Wasserman, 1977 (1977.471)
        Photo: Malcolm Varon

Page 32, DRAGON, *detail from* BENEFICENT RAIN *by Chang Yu-Tsai (d.1316), Chinese handscroll, ink on silk (10 5/8" × 106 3/4")*
    Courtesy of the Metropolitan Museum of Art, Gift of Douglas Dillon, 1985 (1985.227.2)

Page 34, THE FOUR SEASONS—WINTER, OR THE FLOOD, *by Nicolas Poussin (1594–1665), oil on canvas*
    Courtesy of the Louvre, Paris
        Photo: Kavaler/Art Resource, NY

Page 37, HADES, *detail from an Etruscan fresco (ca. 310–300 B.C.)*
        Photo: Art Resource, NY

Page 39, *Detail from* HUNTING SCENE *by Piero di Cosimo (1462–1521), tempera and oil on wood (27 3/4" × 66 3/4")*
    Courtesy of the Metropolitan Museum of Art, Gift of Robert Gordon, 1875 (75.7.2)

Page 41, *Detail from* THE BATTLE OF ISSUS, OR BATTLE OF ALEXANDER AND THE PERSIANS *(1st century B.C.), Mosaic copy from Pompeii (8' 11" × 16' 9 1/2")*
    Courtesy of the National Museum, Naples
        Photo: Scala/Art Resource, NY

Page 42, SHIELD FLANKED BY YOUTHS, *central detail from* THE LEWKNOR ARMORIAL TABLE CARPET, *16th century tapestry, wool and silk (whole: 7' 6" × 16' 4")*
    Courtesy of the Metropolitan Museum of Art, The Fletcher Fund, 1959 (59.33)

Page 45, VESPASIAN *(ca. 75), Roman marble, life-size*
    Courtesy of the National Museum, Naples
        Photo: Art Resource, NY

Page 47, EMOTIONAL SEASONS *(1943) by Gerome Kamrowski, gouache collage and paper on board (21 1/2" × 21 1/8")*

Courtesy of Collection of the Whitney Museum of American Art, NY. Gift of Charles Simon 78.69

Page 50, ORPHEUS CHARMING THE ANIMALS *(1985) by Earl Staley, acrylic on canvas (60" × 54")*
Courtesy of the artist

Page 53, BUMBLEBEE *(1987) by Sally Vagliano, pastel on paper (96" × 94")*
Courtesy of Katharina Rich Perlow Gallery, NY

Page 54, LOTUS FLOWER, *from the T'ang dynasty (618–906), gilt bronze (h. 4" without stand)*
Courtesy of the Metropolitan Museum of Art, Rogers Fund, 1922 (22.79.IIa,b)

Page 56, LANDSCAPE *by A. Everdingen (1621–75), oil on canvas*
Courtesy of the Herzog Anton Ulrich Museum, Brunswick
Photo: Art Resource, NY

Page 58, DAGGER *with hilt in the form of a Nilgai Mughal (mid-17th century), jade and steel (l. 15")*
Courtesy of the Metropolitan Museum of Art, Gift of Nasli Heeramaneck, 1985 (1985.58a)

Page 61, *Detail from* HUNTING SCENE *by Piero di Cosimo, tempera and oil on wood (27 3/4" × 66 3/4")*
Courtesy of the Metropolitan Museum of Art, Gift of Robert Gordon, 1875 (75.7.2)

Page 63, BOY WITH ARROW *by Giorgione (1478–1510), oil on canvas*
Courtesy of Kunsthistorisches Museum, Vienna
Photo: Alinari/Art Resource, NY

Page 64, COOL NOTE *by Adolph Gottlieb (1903–74), oil on canvas (48" × 36")*
Courtesy of the Metropolitan Museum of Art, Gift of the Longview Foundation, in memory of Audrey Stern Hess, 1975 (1975.189.4)

Page 67, LIZARDS ENTWINED IN FOLIAGE *(late 12th century), bronze mirror case (dia. 4 3/8")*
Courtesy of the Metropolitan Museum of Art, the Cloisters Collection, 1947 (47.101.47)
Photo: Lynton Gardiner

Page 70, DYING GAUL, *Roman copy after a bronze original of 230–220 B.C., marble life-size*
Courtesy of the Capitoline Museum, Rome
Photo: Scala/Art Resource, NY

Page 72, VORTEX *(1966) by Harold Tovish, bronze (66" × 18")*
Courtesy of Collection of the Whitney Museum of American Art, NY. Purchase, with funds from an anonymous donor 66.132

Pages 76–77, CORTEO IMPERIALE CON AGRIPPA *(ca. 1st century B.C.–1st century A.D.), Roman bas relief*
Photo: Scala/Art Resource, NY

Page 78, CANTORIA *by Luca Della Robbia (ca. 1400–1482), marble relief*
Courtesy of the Museo dell'Opera, Florence
Photo: Scala/Art Resource, NY

Page 80, UNTITLED *(1988) by Denis Riviere, oil on canvas (76 3/4" × 51 1/4")*
Courtesy of the Maximilian Gallery, NY

# BOOKS BY BERNARD EVSLIN

Merchants of Venus
Heroes, Gods and Monsters of the Greek Myths
Greeks Bearing Gifts: The Epics of Achilles and Ulysses
The Dolphin Rider
Gods, Demigods and Demons
The Green Hero
Heraclea
Signs & Wonders: Tales of the Old Testament